General Knowledge Olympiad

Class 02

A must have book for all
Olympiads & Talent Search Exams...

by
Taru Kaushik

BLOOM CAP
Bloom Cap Edu Ventures Pvt. Ltd.

Bloom Cap Edu Ventures Pvt. Ltd.

✵ **Administrative & Production Office**

'Ramchhaya' 4577/15, Agarwal Road, Darya Ganj, New Delhi -110002
Tele: 011- 47630600, 43518550

✵ **ISBN :** 978-93-25519-41-1

✵ **PRICE :** ₹100.00

✵ **PO No :** TXT-XX-XXXXXXX-X-XX

For further information about the books log on to
www.bloomcap.org

Follow us on   

Preface

"Future belongs to those Who prepares for it today"

School Olympiads are National & International level competitions conducted by different Government, Non-Government & Educational Organisations with the purpose of making the children ready to face competitive exams.

The challenging Questions asked in Olympiads motivate them to learn more & more and bring out the best result with improved academic performance. The Awards & Scholarship offered by Olympiads motivate children to aspire & strive for doing better and emerge out to be the best.

GK Olympiads

GK is the knowledge of every aspect of the human life, which may or may not be the part of routine academic studies but very important for the overall personality development of the students. It is more or less connected with the attentiveness and awareness. There can be different domains of GK like; History, Geography, Polity, Culture, Discovery, Sports, Current Affairs etc.

GK Olympiads help students in understanding the importance of General Knowledge and updations about National & International Affairs in daily life..

'Bloom GK Olympiad Study Book Class 2' is a perfect resource to Study & Practice for Olympiad Exams and other National & State Level Talent Search Exams & Other Competitions.

Some Special Features of Bloom GK Olympiad Study Books are;

- Complete coverage of all the topics related to GK;. Geography, Environment, Polity, Culture, Sports, etc.
- Chapterwise Exercises having different types of Objective Questions.
- Olympiad Pattern Practice Sets at the end.

This book is prepared by Expert Panel with the utmost care, still if you have any suggestions regarding its improvement then feel free to contact us at olympiads@bloomcap.org. We will try to inculcate your suggestions in the further editions.

Contents

Our Surroundings

1. Which one of the following is mismatched?
   (a) Hindu-Temple
   (b) Sikh-Gurudwara
   (c) Muslim-Church
   (d) Muslim-Mosque

2. Which place is used to send and receive letters?
   (a) Police station
   (b) Hospital
   (c) Fire station
   (d) Post office

3. Who makes clays pots and diyas?
   (a) Mechanic
   (b) Carpenter
   (c) Potter
   (d) Plumber

4. Who sells medicines and bandages?
   (a) Doctor
   (b) Nurse
   (c) Chemist
   (d) Fireman

5. We go to which place enjoy tasty food with our family and friends?
   (a) School
   (b) Restaurant
   (c) Park
   (d) Market

6. Who enforce rules and regulates movement of cars and bikes on roads?
   (a) Traffic Policeman
   (b) Servant
   (c) Doctor
   (d) Postman

7. At which of the following places we go to buy variety of things, which we need everyday?
   (a) Police Station
   (b) Market
   (c) Park
   (d) Restaurant

8. Rahul's mother has one brother, Sohan. What is the relation of Sohan with Rahul?
   (a) Cousin
   (b) Maternal uncle
   (c) Brother
   (d) Grandfather

9. In which of the following places you will go to play with your friends?
   (a) School
   (b) Park
   (c) Temple
   (d) Bank

10. How policeman helps us?
   (a) Protects us from robbers and thieves
   (b) Helps us in studies
   (c) Collects garbage
   (d) Sells fruits and vegetables

11. Who protects us from enemy on the borders?
   (a) Plumber
   (b) Servant
   (c) Doctor
   (d) Armyman

12. Which one of the following you will find in hospital?
   (a) Doctor
   (b) Teacher
   (c) Nurse
   (d) Both (a) and (c)

13. Who makes railings and iron gates?
   (a) Tailor
   (b) Green grocers
   (c) Blacksmith
   (d) Chemist

14. In which of the following places we go to deposit our money and take it out when required?
   (a) Bank
   (b) School
   (c) Doctor
   (d) Fire Station

15. The given equipment is used by which of the following?

   (a) Cobbler
   (b) Dentist
   (c) Plumber
   (d) Painter

16. What is my relation with my Paternal uncle's father?
   (a) Grandson
   (b) Nephew
   (c) Cousin
   (d) Uncle

17. Which one of the following you will not find in your school?
   (a) Teacher
   (b) Classmates
   (c) Principal
   (d) Farmer

18. Whose job is to put out fire and save us from getting burnt?
(a) Mechanic
(b) Potter
(c) Astronaut
(d) Fireman

19. Which one of the following tasks is performed by carpenter?
(a) He washes our clothes
(b) He repairs our cars
(c) He repairs our furniture
(d) He stitches our clothes

20. It is the duty of the .... to take care of the patient and give proper treatment.
(a) Tailor
(b) Doctor
(c) Cobbler
(d) Postman

21. If you go to a bakery shop near your house, what products you will get there?
(a) Bread
(b) Biscuits
(c) Cakes
(d) All of these

22. Which one of the following tools is used by tailor?
(a) Hammer
(b) Nails
(c) Scissors
(d) Gun

23. Match the following.

List I (People)		**List II** (Work)
A. Tailor	1.	Sells vegetables
B. Cobbler	2.	Repairs automobiles
C. Mechanic	3.	Mends shoes
D. Grocer	4.	Stitches clothes

Codes

	A	B	C	D			A	B	C	D
(a)	4	3	2	1		(b)	3	4	1	2
(c)	2	3	4	1		(d)	1	2	3	4

Chapter 02

Solar System

1. Which is the 8th planet of our solar system?
   (a) Jupiter
   (c) Mars
   (b) Neptune
   (d) Earth

2. Which one of the following planets is the outer planet of solar system?
   (a) Venus
   (c) Mercury
   (b) Uranus
   (d) Mars

3. Which one of the following planets is known as Evening/Morning Star?
   (a) Earth
   (c) Venus
   (b) Saturn
   (d) Jupiter

4. What is the main feature of planet Jupiter?
   (a) It is the smallest planet
   (c) It is not a planet
   (b) It is the biggest planet
   (d) None of these

5. The smallest planet of our solar system is ....
   (a) Mercury
   (c) Earth
   (b) Venus
   (d) Mars

6. Which one of the following planets is known as Red Planet?
   (a) Jupiter
   (c) Mercury
   (b) Saturn
   (d) Mars

7. Which of the following planets are considered as Twin's ?
   (a) Mercury and Venus
   (c) Earth and Mars
   (b) Venus and Earth
   (d) Mars and Jupiter

8. The path of each planet around the Sun is known as ....
   (a) Orbit
   (c) Revolve
   (b) Axis
   (d) None of these

9. Which one of the following planets is closest to the Sun?
   (a) Mars
   (c) Saturn
   (b) Jupiter
   (d) Mercury

10. Which of the following instruments is used to see the planets?
    (a) Telescope   (b) Microscope
    (c) Kaleidoscope   (d) Camera

11. Which planet of the solar system is surrounded by ring-like structures?
    (a) Mercury   (b) Mars
    (c) Earth   (d) Saturn

12. Find the mismatched pair.
    (a) Mars   Red planet   (b) Jupiter   Largest planet
    (c) Venus   Hottest planet   (d) Earth   Green planet

13. Which planet is also known as winter planet?
    (a) Mars   (b) Earth
    (c) Jupiter   (d) Uranus

14. Which planet is located between Mars and Saturn?
    (a) Jupiter   (b) Mercury
    (c) Earth   (d) Uranus

15. The movement of 365 days of Earth around the Sun is known as ....
    (a) Rotation   (b) Revolution
    (c) Orbit   (d) Axis

16. Which of the following is not a planet?
    (a) Mars   (b) Saturn
    (c) Moon   (d) Venus

17. Which of these planet is smaller than Earth?
    (a) Saturn   (b) Mercury
    (c) Jupiter   (d) All of these

18. Which planet revolves fastest around the Sun?
    (a) Neptune   (b) Uranus
    (c) Jupiter   (d) Mercury

19. We are not able to see the Moon during which phase?
    (a) New Moon   (b) Full Moon
    (c) Crescent Moon   (d) Red Moon

20. Which star is located in the center of the solar system?
    (a) Sun   (b) Moon
    (c) Earth   (d) Jupiter

21. Which of the following is NOT true about the Sun?
    (a) It is closest to Earth.   (b) It is a star.
    (c) It is the source of heat.   (d) It is round in shape.

22. Life is found on how many planets of solar system?

(a) One (b) Two

(c) Five (d) Six

23. Due to which movement of Earth, there is change of seasons?

(a) Rotation (b) Revolution

(c) Spin (d) All of these

24. Which of the following heavenly body has its own light?

(a) Earth (b) Jupiter

(c) Sun (d) Moon

25. Match the following lists correctly.

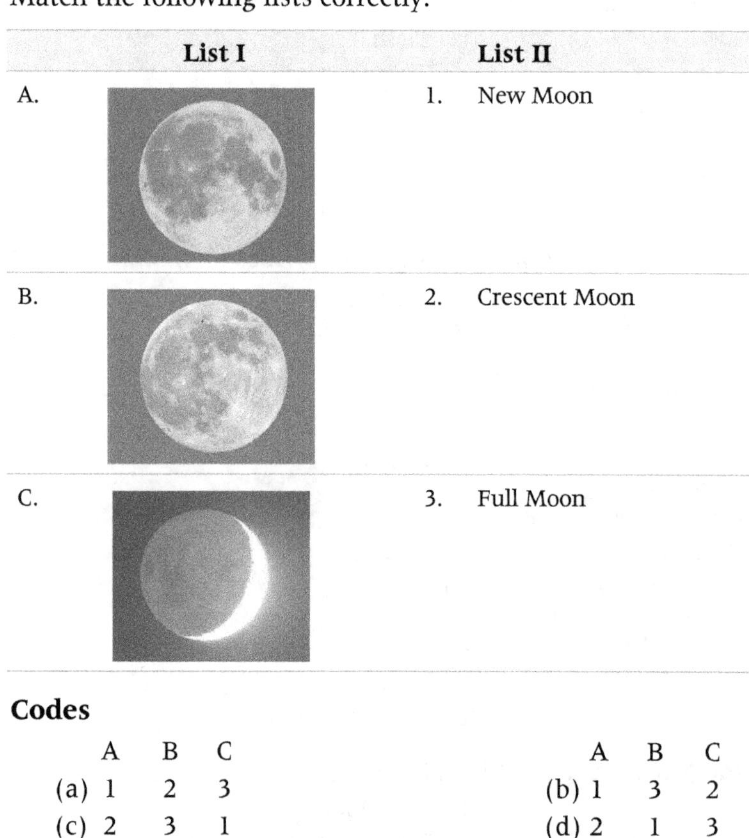

	List I		List II
A.		1.	New Moon
B.		2.	Crescent Moon
C.		3.	Full Moon

Codes

	A	B	C			A	B	C
(a)	1	2	3		(b)	1	3	2
(c)	2	3	1		(d)	2	1	3

Chapter

03

My Country

1. What is the National Anthem of our country?
   (a) Vande Matram
   (b) Jana Gana Mana
   (c) Sare Jahan Se Acha
   (d) None of these

2. Which one of the following is the smallest State of India?
   (a) Rajasthan
   (b) Goa
   (c) Gujarat
   (d) Punjab

3. Which of the following states is located in the Southern part of India?
   (a) Punjab
   (b) Haryana
   (c) Himachal Pradesh
   (d) Andhra Pradesh

4. How many states are present in India since the year 2020?
   (a) 19
   (b) 28
   (c) 30
   (d) 22

5. Chandigarh is the capital of which state?
   (a) Rajasthan
   (b) Delhi
   (c) Punjab
   (d) Uttar Pradesh

6. The state Gujarat is in which direction to West Bengal?
   (a) East
   (b) West
   (c) North
   (d) South

7. The famous market Chandni Chowk is located in which city?
   (a) Jaipur
   (b) Kolkata
   (c) Delhi
   (d) Mumbai

8. Find the odd one out.
   (a) Puducherry
   (b) Chandigarh
   (c) Lakshadweep
   (d) Odisha

9. Which one of the following is the capital of Uttar Pradesh?
   (a) Lucknow
   (b) Prayagraj
   (c) Kanpur
   (d) Agra

10. Which one of the following is the Eastern most state of India?
    (a) Gujarat
    (b) Arunachal Pradesh
    (c) Odisha
    (d) West Bengal

11. Which of the following states of India is popularly known for the production of tea?
    (a) Himachal Pradesh
    (b) Telangana
    (c) Karnataka
    (d) Assam

12. Which of the following cities of India is known as 'Space City of India'?
    (a) New Delhi
    (b) Chennai
    (c) Bengaluru
    (d) Mumbai

13. Which of the following states of India is located in the Western part of India?
    (a) Rajasthan
    (b) Assam
    (c) Sikkim
    (d) Tamil Nadu

14. Which one of the following is the capital city of Madhya Pradesh?
    (a) Bhopal
    (b) Jabalpur
    (c) Indore
    (d) Gwalior

15. Which place in India is also known as the "Land of Rising Sun"?
    (a) Sikkim
    (b) Arunachal Pradesh
    (c) Karnataka
    (d) Gujarat

16. The city Mumbai is also known as ....
    (a) City of Dreams
    (b) Hollywood of India
    (c) City of Palaces
    (d) Both (a) and (b)

17. Ranchi is the capital of which state?
    (a) Rajasthan
    (b) Sikkim
    (c) Uttar Pradesh
    (d) Jharkhand

18. In which of the following states language Malayalam is spoken by the people?
    (a) Bihar
    (b) Chhattisgarh
    (c) West Bengal
    (d) Kerala

19. In which of the following zones of India, the seven sister states are located?
    (a) South zone
    (b) North zone
    (c) East zone
    (d) West zone

20. Which of the following Union Territory is also the capital of Haryana?
    (a) Daman and Diu
    (b) Ladakh
    (c) Delhi
    (d) Chandigarh

21. Which one of the following cities is the capital of Himachal Pradesh?
    (a) Shimla
    (b) Kufri
    (c) Dharamshala
    (d) Mussoorie

22. The famous Marine Drive is located in which city?
    (a) Kolkata
    (b) Bengaluru
    (c) Chennai
    (d) Mumbai

23. Which state is known as Sugar Bowl of India?
    (a) Gujarat
    (b) Rajasthan
    (c) Uttar Pradesh
    (d) Madhya Pradesh

24. In which of the following states, the tallest Statue of India is located?
    (a) Manipur
    (b) West Bengal
    (c) Odisha
    (d) Gujarat

25. Find the mismatched pair.

	State	Capital
(a)	Uttar Pradesh	Lucknow
(b)	Tamil Nadu	Chennai
(c)	Maharashtra	Nagpur
(d)	Uttarakhand	Dehradun

Our President, PMs and CMs

1. Who is the first Prime Minister of India?
   (a) Mahatma Gandhi
   (b) Sardar Vallabhbhai Patel
   (c) Subhas Chandra Bose
   (d) Jawaharlal Nehru

2. Indira Gandhi was the .... women Prime Minister of India.
   (a) First
   (b) Second
   (c) Third
   (d) Fourth

3. Which of the following former President was also a scientist?
   (a) Ram Nath Kovind
   (b) Pranab Mukherjee
   (c) Pratibha Patil
   (d) APJ Abdul Kalam

4. Who was the first women President of India?
   (a) Indira Gandhi
   (b) Sarojini Naidu
   (c) Annie Besant
   (d) Pratibha Patil

5. Dr. Rajendra Prasad was elected as first .... of India.
   (a) Prime Minister
   (b) Chief Minister
   (c) President
   (d) Both (a) and (c)

6. Which of the following Prime Minister gave the slogan 'Jai Jawaan Jai Kisaan'?
   (a) Jawaharlal Nehru
   (b) Indira Gandhi
   (c) Lal Bahadur Shastri
   (d) Narendra Modi

7. Which one of the following has never become the Prime Minister of India?
   (a) Rajiv Gandhi
   (b) Atal Bihari Vajpayee
   (c) Manmohan Singh
   (d) Pranab Mukherjee

8. Who was the first Vice-President of India?
   (a) Rajendra Prasad
   (b) A P J Abdul Kalam
   (c) Sarvepalli Radhakrishnan
   (d) Sardar Patel

9. Who is the present Chief Minister of Maharashtra?
   (a) Amarinder Singh
   (b) Uddhav Thackeray
   (c) Mamata Banerjee
   (d) Yogi Adityanath

10. The personality shown in the picture is the Chief Minister of which state?

(a) Gujarat   (b) West Bengal
(c) Punjab   (d) Uttar Pradesh

11. Identify the personality shown in the picture.

(a) Manmohan Singh   (b) Rajnath Singh
(c) Sanjay Gandhi   (d) Charan Singh

12. Which is India's youngest Prime Minister?
(a) Narendra Modi   (b) Rajiv Gandhi
(c) Atal Bihari Vajpayee   (d) Indira Gandhi

13. Identify the personality shown in the picture.

(a) Narendra Modi   (b) Atal Bihari Vajpayee
(c) Lal Bahadur Shastri   (d) Sardar Patel

14. Which one of the following has served as the President of India?
(a) Zakir Hussain   (b) Sonia Gandhi
(c) Nitish Kumar   (d) Sanjay Gandhi

15. Identify the personality shown in the picture.

(a) Yogi Adityanath   (b) Arvind Kejriwal
(c) MK Stalin   (d) Uddhav Thackeray

16. Which of the following is the current Vice-President of India?
(a) Zakir Hussain   (b) M. Hamid Ansari
(c) M. Venkaiah Naidu   (d) Naveen Patnaik

17. Which one of the following is the youngest Chief Minister of any state of India?
(a) Akhilesh Yadav   (b) Sachin Pilot
(c) Amarinder Singh   (d) Pema Khandu

18. Narendra Modi is serving as the .... Prime Minister of India.
(a) 12th   (b) 13th
(c) 14th   (d) 15th

Country ,
Capital and Flag

1. Which one of the following is the neighbouring country of India?
   (a) USA
   (b) Iran
   (c) Nepal
   (d) United Kingdom

2. The given flag belongs to which of the following country?

   (a) United States of America
   (b) Canada
   (c) France
   (d) United Kingdom

3. The flag shown in the image belongs to which country?
   Hint : Its capital is Canberra

   (a) Japan
   (b) China
   (c) Thailand
   (d) Australia

4. Which one of the following is the capital of Japan?
   (a) Tokyo
   (b) London
   (c) Paris
   (d) Dhaka

5. Which one of the following is the capital of Afghanistan?
   (a) Abu Dhabi   (b) Kabul
   (c) Dhaka   (d) Beijing

6. Which one of the following is the capital of Canada?
   (a) Beijing   (b) Ottawa
   (c) Paris   (d) Colombo

7. Beijing is the capital of ....
   (a) Bangladesh   (b) Bhutan
   (c) China   (d) Nepal

8. Identify the Country from the flag given below.

   (a) USA   (b) United Kingdom
   (c) Australia   (d) Israel

9. Find the odd one out from the given options.
   (a) Moscow   (b) USA
   (c) UK   (d) Australia

10. Identify the country from the given flag.

   (a) Bangladesh   (b) Sri Lanka
   (c) Australia   (d) Pakistan

11. The given flag in the picture is representing, which of the following country?

(a) China   (b) Japan
(c) Bangladesh   (d) France

12. Madrid is the capital of which country?
(a) Spain   (b) France
(c) Germany   (d) USA

13. The Pyramids shown in the picture are located in which country?

(a) Jamaica   (b) Saudi Arabia
(c) Egypt   (d) Turkey

14. Which one of the following is the capital of Italy?
(a) Colombo   (b) Islamabad
(c) Rome   (d) Berlin

15. The given flag is the national flag of which of the following country?

(a) USA   (b) UK
(c) Australia   (d) China

16. Which one of the following is the capital of France?
    (a) Beijing   (b) London
    (c) Paris   (d) Manila

17. The building shown in the picture is in which country?

    (a) Germany   (b) France
    (c) Italy   (d) USA

18. If "U.S.A" is related to "WASHINGTON DC" then, "U.K" is related to "   "?
    (a) New York   (b) Florida
    (c) London   (d) Wales

19. Which one of the following pairs of "COUNTRY-CAPITAL" is not correctly matched?
    (a) Pakistan-Islamabad   (b) Nepal-Kathmandu
    (c) China-Beijing   (d) Myanmar-Dhaka

Chapter

06

Fairs, Festivals and Religion

1. Which one of the following is the harvest festival celebrated in Kerala?
   (a) Onam
   (b) Hornbill
   (c) Bihu
   (d) Pongal

2. Pongal is celebrated in which of the following states?
   (a) Punjab
   (b) Odisha
   (c) Madhya Pradesh
   (d) Tamil Nadu

3. Which one of the following is not a National Festival of India?
   (a) Independence Day
   (b) Baisakhi
   (c) Gandhi Jayanti
   (d) Republic Day

4. Which of the following is a religious festival?
   (a) Republic Day
   (b) Christmas
   (c) Eid
   (d) Both (b) and (c)

5. Gudi Parwa and Ganesh Chaturthi are the famous festivals of which of the following states?
   (a) Uttar Pradesh
   (b) Karnataka
   (c) Punjab
   (d) Maharashtra

6. Which one of the following festivals is celebrated in the state Assam?
   (a) Bihu
   (b) Baisakhi
   (c) Losar
   (d) Bundi

7. The famous festival 'Hornbill' is celebrated in which of the following states?
   (a) Uttarakhand
   (b) Haryana
   (c) Nagaland
   (d) Rajasthan

8. Which one of the following is a place of worship?
   (a) Mosque
   (b) Church
   (c) Gurudwara
   (d) All of these

9. Which one of the following fairs is held in Rajasthan every year?
   (a) Kumbh Mela
   (b) Pushkar Mela
   (c) Hornbill Mela
   (d) Craft Mela

10. Which one of the following festivals is celebrated as the birth of Jesus Christ?
    (a) Raksha Bandhan
    (b) Dusshera
    (c) Christmas
    (d) Republic Day

11. Quran is the holy book of which religion?
    (a) Christians
    (b) Muslims
    (c) Hindus
    (d) Parsis

12. Which one of the following festivals is celebrated by Muslims at the end of the fasting month of Ramadan?
    (a) Durga Puja
    (b) Eid
    (c) Good Friday
    (d) Diwali

13. Which one of the following festival is the symbol of love between brother and sister?
    (a) Dusshera
    (b) Holi
    (c) Raksha Bandhan
    (d) Christmas

14. Which God is worshipped the occasion of Janmashtami?
    (a) Lord Hanuman
    (b) Lord Ganesha
    (c) Lord Ram
    (d) Lord Krishna

15. Durga Puja is the main festival of which state?
    (a) Karnataka
    (b) West Bengal
    (c) Punjab
    (d) Uttarakhand

16. Which of these festival is celebrated in Punjab?
    (a) Durga Puja
    (b) Dussehra
    (c) Lohri
    (d) Holi

17. Which of the following festival is celebrated as "Victory of good over evil"?
    (a) Diwali
    (b) Dusshera
    (c) Holi
    (d) Christmas

18. Our Muslim friends go to Mosque ....
    (a) to sleep
    (b) to pray
    (c) to eat the food
    (d) to worship the God

19. Which one of the following is the first Guru of Sikh community?
    (a) Guru Nanak
    (b) Guru Gobind Singh
    (c) Guru Arjan Dev
    (d) Gurudev

20. The Ramayana and the Mahabharata are the epic books of which religion?
   (a) Sikhism
   (b) Hinduism
   (c) Islam
   (d) Christianity

21. Which one of the following is the holy book of the Christians?
   (a) Avesta
   (b) Guru Granth Sahib
   (c) Bible
   (d) Bhagvad Gita

22. The city Prayagraj, Ujjain and Haridwar is famous for which of the following fairs?
   (a) Pushkar Mela
   (b) Craft Mela
   (c) Kumbh Mela
   (d) Chhath Puja

23. The Rath Yatra in Puri is the famous, festival celebrated in which of the following states?
   (a) Jammu and Kashmir
   (b) Karnataka
   (c) West Bengal
   (d) Odisha

24. In which of the following states, Surajkund Mela, the World's Largest International Crafts Fair held ?
   (a) Uttar Pradesh
   (b) Rajasthan
   (c) Haryana
   (d) Maharashtra

25. During which National festival, parades are held at India Gate?
   (a) Independence Day
   (b) Republic Day
   (c) Gandhi Jayanti
   (d) None of these

26. The Holi festival celebrated every year is considered as........... .
   (a) festival of Joy
   (b) festival of Colours
   (c) festival of Light
   (d) festival of War

27. Which one of the following is the holy place of Muslims?
   (a) Golden Temple
   (b) Kedarnath Temple
   (c) Mecca-Madina
   (d) Shimla Christ Church

28. Which one of the following Hindu Goddess is known as Goddess of learning, wisdom and music?
   (a) Maa Laxmi
   (b) Maa Durga
   (c) Maa Saraswati
   (d) Maa Kali

Music and Dance

1. Which of these musical instrument is played by using only fingers?
   - (a) Drum
   - (b) Piano
   - (c) Flute
   - (d) Trumpet

2. Garba and Dandiya Rass are the famous dance forms of which of the following states?
   - (a) Rajasthan
   - (b) Uttar Pradesh
   - (c) Karnataka
   - (d) Gujarat

3. Which one of the following is a wind instrument?
   - (a) Sitar
   - (b) Flute
   - (c) Drum
   - (d) Tabla

4. The classical dance Kathakali belongs to which of the following states?
   - (a) Maharashtra
   - (b) Rajasthan
   - (c) Kerala
   - (d) Madhya Pradesh

5. How many notes of Sur are present in Hindustani music?
   - (a) 7
   - (b) 8
   - (c) 6
   - (d) 9

6. Which of the following are the famous dances of the state Punjab?
   - (a) Giddha
   - (b) Bhangra
   - (c) Lavani
   - (d) Both (a) and (b)

7. What is the name of the instrument usually depicted holding or playing by Goddess Saraswati?
   - (a) Guitar
   - (b) Sitar
   - (c) Violin
   - (d) Veena

8. AR Rahman is a famous ....
   - (a) Dancer
   - (b) Musician
   - (c) Actor
   - (d) Director

9. Find the odd one out from the given music instruments.
   - (a) Tabla
   - (b) Guitar
   - (c) Sitar
   - (d) Veena

10. Which one of the following is the famous dance form of Tamil Nadu?
    (a) Ghoomar   (b) Bharatanatyam
    (c) Garba   (d) Bhangra

11. Identify the given instruments.

    (a) Tabla   (b) Harmonium   (c) Sitar   (d) Flute

12. Which one of the following is the famous dance form of the state Maharashtra?
    (a) Ghoomar   (b) Kuchipudi   (c) Giddha   (d) Lavani

13. 'Kuchipudi' is a ....
    (a) Dance   (b) Musical instrument
    (c) Song   (d) None of these

14. The dance shown in the image is ....

    (a) Kuchipudi   (b) Bhangra
    (c) Kathak   (d) Bharatanatyam

15. Identify the famous singer shown in the picture.

    (a) Shaan   (b) Arman Malik
    (c) Udit Narayan   (d) Sonu Nigam

16. Which of these instrument does not have strings?
    (a) Harmonium   (b) Guitar
    (c) Violin   (d) Veena

17. The JHUMAR dance form belongs to which of the following states?
    (a) Uttar Pradesh   (b) Haryana
    (c) Madhya Pradesh   (d) Odisha

18. Which one of the following is not a musical instrument?
    (a) Harmonium   (b) Spanner
    (c) Flute   (d) Trumpet

19. Which one of the following instruments is played by famous Indian Musician Ustad Zakir Hussain?
    (a) Flute   (b) Guitar
    (c) Tabla   (d) Violin

20. Which one of the following is the famous dance form of the state Rajasthan?
    (a) Ghoomar   (b) Mohiniyattam
    (c) Kathak   (d) Kuchipudi

21. Find out the missing Raag, which consists of seven notes?

    Sa, Re, Ga,__, Pa, Dha, Ni.
    (a) Dha   (b) Ma
    (c) Ni   (d) Ra

22. The famous dance form Manipuri is a famous dance form of which state?
    (a) Mizoram   (b) Tripura
    (c) Meghalaya   (d) Manipur

23. What is the name of the famous musician who played "SHEHNAI"?
    (a) Ustad Bismillah Khan (b) Ustad Zakir Hussain
    (c) Shiv Kumar Sharma   (d) Arijit Singh

24. Identify the given musical instrument in the picture.

    (a) Mouth organ   (b) Flute
    (c) Shehnai   (d) Violin

25. Find the odd one out.
    (a) Kirtan   (b) Qawwali
    (c) Ghazal   (d) Violin

Chapter 08

Famous Places

1. Which one of the following monuments will you NOT find in New Delhi?
   (a) Taj Mahal
   (b) Red Fort
   (c) Qutub Minar
   (d) Jantar Mantar

2. The famous monument shown in the picture is located in which state?

   (a) Haryana
   (b) Odisha
   (c) Delhi
   (d) Punjab

3. Which one of the following monument is one of the wonders of the world?
   (a) India Gate
   (b) Lotus Temple
   (c) Taj Mahal
   (d) Gateway of India

4. In which of the following city, The Gateway of India is located?
   (a) Delhi
   (b) Kolkata
   (c) Chennai
   (d) Mumbai

5. Identify the given monument.

   (a) Char Minar
   (b) Lotus Temple
   (c) Hawa Mahal
   (d) Gateway of India

6. What is the name of the world's talleststatue located in Gujarat?
   (a) Mahatma Gandhi Statue　　(b) Statue of Freedom
   (c) Statue of Liberty　　(d) Statue of Unity

7. Which one of the following monuments is a Tall tower?
   (a) Taj Mahal　　(b) India Gate
   (c) Jantar Mantar　　(d) Qutub Minar

8. Which of the following monuments is located in the city of Hyderabad?
   (a) Taj Mahal　　(b) Buland Darwaza
   (c) Gateway of India　　(d) Char Minar

9. On which of the following monuments our Prime Minister hoists the flag on Independence Day?
   (a) Jantar Mantar　　(b) India Gate
   (c) Red Fort　　(d) Akshardham Temple

10. Which one of the following monuments was built to pay tribute to the soldiers died in World War-I?
    (a) India Gate　　(b) Qutub Minar
    (c) Char Minar　　(d) Taj Mahal

11. Which of the following temples is located in Amritsar, Punjab?
    (a) Lotus Temple　　(b) Birla Temple
    (c) Akshardham Temple　　(d) Golden Temple

12. In which of the following states, Agra Fort is located?
    (a) New Delhi　　(b) Rajasthan　　(c) Haryana　　(d) Uttar Pradesh

13. The official residence of our President is known as............ .
    (a) Parliament　　(b) Taj Mahal
    (c) Rashtrapati Bhawan　　(d) Lok Sabha

14. In which of the following States/Union Territory the famous "Rock Garden" is located?
    (a) Telangana　　(b) Puducherry　　(c) Chandigarh　　(d) Punjab

15. Identify the famous building shown in the picture.

    (a) Rashtrapati Bhawan　　(b) Parliament
    (c) India Gate　　(d) Delhi Gate

16. Which one of the following cities is known as city of lakes?
    (a) Jaipur (b) Udaipur
    (c) Mumbai (d) Nagpur

17. Which of the following place is famous as Heaven on Earth?
    (a) Kashmir (b) Shimla
    (c) Mussoorie (d) Udaipur

18. In which of the following cities the famous Sun Temple is located?
    (a) Konark (b) Sambalpur
    (c) Rourkela (d) Belgaum

19. Which one of the following city is famous as Pink City?
    (a) Jaipur (b) Agra
    (c) Udaipur (d) Mathura

20. In which of the following states the biggest cricket stadium is located?
    (a) Andhra Pradesh (b) Tamil Nadu
    (c) Punjab (d) Gujarat

21. The pilgrimage(s) located in Uttarakhand is/are............. .
    (a) Haridwar (b) Kedarnath
    (c) Badrinath (d) All of these

22. Which famous monument is NOT located in Uttar Pradesh?
    (a) Taj Mahal (b) Agra Fort
    (c) Sanchi Stupa (d) Buland Darwaza

23. Shimla, Nainital, Mussoorie are famous ....
    (a) Beaches (b) Hill Stations
    (c) Monuments (d) Cities

24. The mosque "Jama Masjid" is located in which of the following cities?
    (a) New Delhi (b) Haridwar
    (c) Mussoorie (d) Nainital

Human Body

1. Which one of the following is NOT a part of hands?
   (a) Knee   (b) Arm
   (c) Wrist   (d) Elbow

2. Which of the following organ protects us from external environment and germs?
   (a) Tongue   (b) Skin
   (c) Teeth   (d) Eyes

3. Which of the following organ helps in breathing?
   (a) Lungs   (b) Heart
   (c) Stomach   (d) Brain

4. Every human being has one .... to taste different food items.
   (a) Hand   (b) Leg
   (c) Eye   (d) Tongue

5. Which body part helps us to smell our favourite food?
   (a) Nose   (b) Ears
   (c) Eyes   (d) Tongue

6. We cannot see anything, without which sense organs?
   (a) Ears   (b) Brain
   (c) Eyes   (d) Heart

7. Which organ helps in blood circulation in the body?
   (a) Lungs   (b) Kidney
   (c) Nose   (d) Heart

8. Which of the following sense organ helps us to listen to our teachers?
   (a) Ears   (b) Eyes
   (c) Brain   (d) Heart

9. Which parts of body, regrow again when we cut it?
   (a) Nails   (b) Hairs
   (c) Fingers   (d) Both (a) and (b)

10. Pick the odd one out

(a) 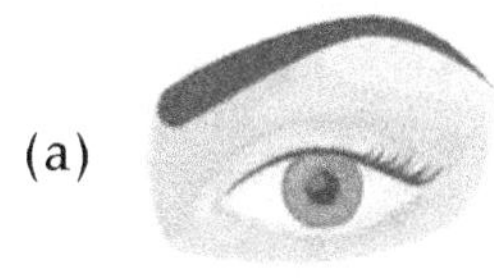

(b) 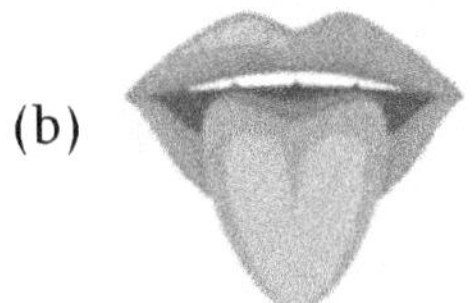

(c) 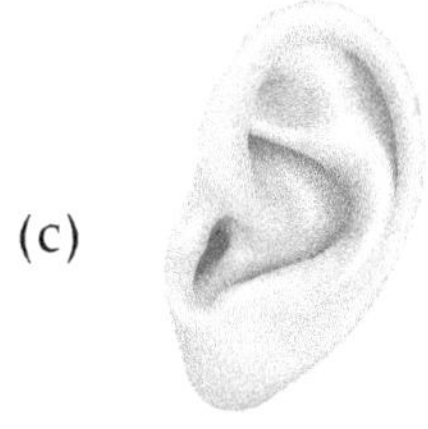

(d) 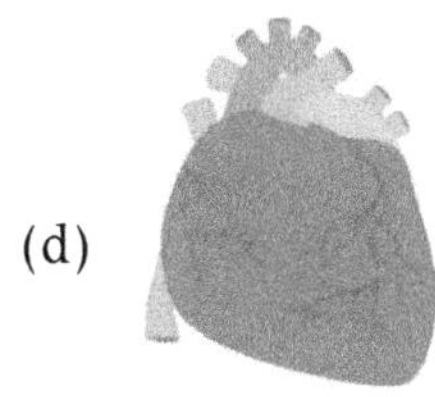

11. Which organ of the body beats faster when we run?
   (a) Brain   (b) Heart
   (c) Legs   (d) Eyes

12. Which one of the following organs helps to think and to take decisions?
   (a) Heart   (b) Kidneys
   (c) Lungs   (d) Brain

13. Which of the following organ breaks the food into pieces in our mouth?
   (a) Tongue   (b) Teeth
   (c) Nails   (d) Lips

14. Which part of the body helps us to lift, throw, push and pull?
   (a) Legs   (b) Heart
   (c) Arms   (d) Knees

15. Which one of the following is a sense organ?
   (a) Kidneys   (b) Brain   (c) Lungs   (d) Skin

16. The body part shown in the picture performs which function?

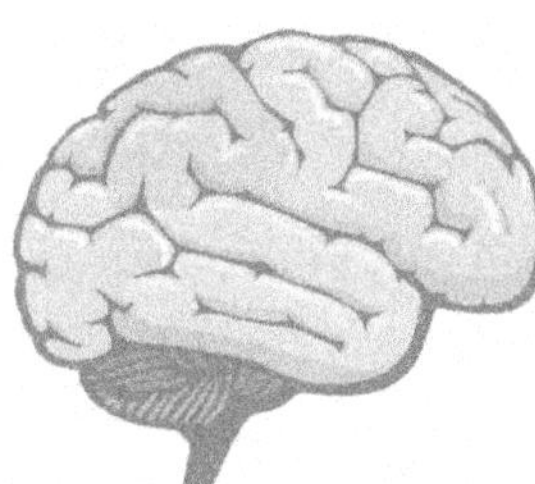

   (a) Take decisions   (b) Learn the school work
   (c) Think about our friends   (d) All of these

17. Which part of the body is not present in a pair?
(a) Lungs
(b) Kidneys
(c) Heart
(d) Ears

18. The Lungs are located inside which of the following parts?
(a) Legs
(b) Brain
(c) Mouth
(d) Chest

19. What is the work done by stomach in our body?
(a) To provide oxygen
(b) To circulate the blood
(c) To listen
(d) To digest the food

20. Which of the following part of human body is a Memory keeper?
(a) Heart
(b) Brain
(c) Hands
(d) Tongue

21. Which of the following is an internal organ?
(a) Kidneys
(b) Palm
(c) Nose
(d) Chest

22. Match the following.

List I (Body Parts)		List II (Located At)
A. Nails	1.	Hands
B. Ears	2.	Legs
C. Foot	3.	Head
D. Wrist	4.	Fingers

Codes

	A	B	C	D		A	B	C	D
(a)	1	2	3	4	(b)	2	3	4	1
(c)	3	4	1	2	(d)	4	3	2	1

23. How many bones are there in human body?
(a) 206
(b) 310
(c) 115
(d) 76

24. Which one of the following is the soft part of our body?
(a) Teeth
(b) Bones
(c) Muscles
(d) None of these

Chapter 10

Food

1. Among the given nutrients, milk is considered as a good source of ....
   (a) Calcium
   (b) Vitamin B
   (c) Carbohydrate
   (d) Vitamin C

2. Which of the following is considered a complete protein food?
   (a) Almond
   (b) Turmeric
   (c) Soybean
   (d) Amla

3. Which of the following nutrients is needed for a healthy immune system?
   (a) Calcium
   (b) Iodine
   (c) Vitamin K
   (d) Vitamin C

4. Pulses are a good source of ....
   (a) Carbohydrates
   (b) Proteins
   (c) Fats
   (d) Vitamins

5. Which of the following is not considered as Junk Food?
   (a) Burger
   (b) Pizza
   (c) Oats
   (d) Noodles

6. Which of the following food items is made from milk?
   (a) Fish
   (b) Potato
   (c) Cheese
   (d) Egg

7. Which of the following food comes from the leaves of a plant?
   (a) Spinach
   (b) Mango
   (c) Potato
   (d) Rice

8. Which of the following food can be eaten only after cooking it properly?
   (a) Cucumber
   (b) Rice
   (c) Radish
   (d) Apple

9. Which of the following is true?
   (a) Food gives us energy and helps us to grow.
   (b) We cannot eat apple without cooking.
   (c) We should live in dirty house only.
   (d) We should not eat fruits and vegetables daily.

10. Which of these food is obtained from animals?
    (a) Egg
    (b) Milk
    (c) Meat
    (d) All of these

11. Which of the following minerals helps us to build strong bones and teeth?
(a) Iodine
(b) Calcium
(c) Iron
(d) Sodium

12. Which of the following food components does not provide any nutrients?
(a) Milk
(b) Water
(c) Fruit Juice
(d) Vegetable soup

13. Which of the following food components is rich in fat?
(a) Rice and Maize
(b) Milk, egg and beans
(c) Butter, cheese and oil
(d) None of these

14. Guava, Lemon, Orange and Tomato are rich in ....
(a) Vitamin A
(b) Vitamin B
(c) Vitamin C
(d) Vitamin D

15. Which of these can be eaten raw even without cooking?
(a) Brinjal
(b) Potato
(c) Pumpkin
(d) Carrot

16. The diet that has the right amount of all the nutrients our body needs is called ....
(a) healthy food
(b) balanced diet
(c) fast food
(d) fantastic diet

17. Which of the following food helps us in keeping our muscles strong?
(a) Banana
(b) Eggs
(c) Soup
(d) Pasta

18. Find the odd one out.
(a) Pastry
(b) Potato Chips
(c) Idli
(d) Dough nut

19. Consider the following statements and find true and false (T/F).
A. We should eat only meat to remain healthy.
B. Eating vegetables makes us ill.
(a) A-True, B-False
(b) A-False, B-False
(c) A-True, B-True
(d) A-False, B-True

20. Match the following.

	List I		List II
A.	Orange	1.	River
B.	Sugar	2.	Cow
C.	Milk	3.	Sugarcane
D.	Fish	4.	Plant

Codes

	A	B	C	D			A	B	C	D
(a)	1	3	2	4		(b)	4	3	2	1
(c)	2	3	4	1		(a)	1	2	3	4

Chapter 11

Plants

1. Which one of the following is a tree?
   (a) Neem
   (b) Money plant
   (c) Grapevine
   (d) Tulsi

2. Which one of the following is not a shrub?
   (a) Sun flower plant
   (b) Rose plant
   (c) Guava plant
   (d) Marigold plant

3. Which of the following is not a creeper?
   (a) Watermelon
   (b) Pumpkin
   (c) Strawberry
   (d) Rose

4. Which one of the following parts of plant develops inside the soil?
   (a) Stem
   (b) Leaves
   (c) Root
   (d) Flowers

5. Which among the following is not a plant?
   (a) Rose plant
   (b) Mushroom
   (c) Banana Tree
   (d) Coconut Tree

6. Which one of the following plants does not produce fruits?
   (a) Marigold
   (b) Banana Tree
   (c) Mango Tree
   (d) Coconut Tree

7. Which of the following plants will you normally find in desert area?
   (a) Pineapple
   (b) Rice plant
   (c) Cactus
   (d) Mango tree

8. Which one of the following pairs is not correctly matched?
   (a) Root — Carrot
   (b) Stem — Potato
   (c) Flower — Cauliflower
   (d) Fruit — Cabbage

9. Which one of the following is not a plant product?
   (a) Flower
   (b) Fruit
   (c) Rubber
   (d) Butter

10. The leaves of which plant can be eaten to cure cold and cough?
(a) Rose
(b) Tulsi
(c) Mustard
(d) Apple

11. Find the odd one out.
(a) Apple
(b) Jasmine
(c) Orange
(d) Banana

12. Match the following.

	List I (Plant)		**List II** (Identity)
A.	Sugarcane	1.	To make perfumes
B.	Jasmine	2.	To make medicine
C.	Neem	3.	To make furniture
D.	Bamboos	4.	To make sugar

Codes

	A	B	C	D			A	B	C	D
(a)	4	1	2	3		(b)	1	2	3	4
(c)	2	3	1	4		(d)	3	4	1	2

13. Which of the following vegetable is root of a plant?
(a) Peas
(b) Radish
(c) Tomato
(d) Spinach

14. Which one of the following plant grows in water?
(a) Sunflower
(b) Lotus
(c) Jasmine
(d) None of these

15. Which one of the following is not a example of climber plant?
(a) Pea
(b) Grapevine
(c) Bean
(d) Spinach

16. Find the mismatched.
(a) Herbs– Tomato
(b) Shrubs– Mango Tree
(c) Tree – Banyan
(d) Climber – Bottle gourd or Lauki

17. Which part of plant helps it to absorb water and minerals?
(a) Leaves
(b) Root
(c) Leaf
(d) Flower

18. Find the odd one out.
(a) Jasmine
(b) Lotus
(c) Rose
(d) Cactus

19. Which one of the following part of plant provides support to upper part of plant?
    (a) Root
    (b) Stem
    (c) Lever
    (d) Fruits

20. We get mint from which part of plant?
    (a) Root
    (b) Stem
    (c) Leaves
    (d) Flower

21. Mint, Tulsi, Coriander all are examples of ....
    (a) Stem
    (b) Herbs
    (c) Shrubs
    (d) Seeds

22. Find the odd one out on the basis of their colour.
    (a) Rose – Green
    (b) Sunflower – Yellow
    (c) Brinjal – Purple
    (d) Grass – Green

23. Oil is not obtained from which of the following plants?
    (a) Sunflower plant
    (b) Mustard plant
    (c) Banyan plant
    (d) Coconut plant

24. Fruits, flowers and vegetables grow on many plants, except ....
    (a) Grass
    (b) Mango Tree
    (c) Rose plant
    (d) Pea plant

25. Find the wrong option.
    (a) Tea — Made from dried tea leaves
    (b) Coffee — Made from coffee beans
    (c) Sugar — Made from the juice of sugarcane
    (d) Clove — Made from bamboo

26. Which one of the following has a strong stem?
    (a) Climbers
    (b) Creepers
    (c) Herbs
    (d) Tree

27. Which one of the following is an aquatic plant?
    (a) Mint
    (b) Pumpkin
    (c) Rose
    (d) Water lily

Animals

1. Identify the pair of animals that live in water.
   - (a) Sparrow, Fish
   - (b) Fish, Crocodile
   - (c) Elephant, Snake
   - (d) Monkey, Rabbit

2. Which one of the following is not a bird?
   - (a) Peacock
   - (b) Owl
   - (c) Sparrow
   - (d) Butterfly

3. We obtain honey from which of the following insects?
   - (a) Wasp
   - (b) Butterfly
   - (c) Honeybee
   - (d) Grasshopper

4. You will find .... on tree and .... in water.
   - (a) Snake, Rabbit
   - (b) Monkey, Frog
   - (c) Lion, Tiger
   - (d) Rabbit, Owl

5. How can you identify Giraffe in the Jungle?
   - (a) It has a long neck.
   - (b) It has a big trunk
   - (c) It runs very fast.
   - (d) It lives in water.

6. Which animal makes the Growling sound?
   - (a) Tiger
   - (b) Bear
   - (c) Lion
   - (d) Buffalo

7. Which of the following is not correctly matched?
   - (a) Bear – Cave
   - (b) Horse – Stable
   - (c) Fish – Stable
   - (d) Dog – Kennel

8. The baby of a Horde is known as ....
   - (a) Kid
   - (b) Cub
   - (c) Calf
   - (d) Foal

9. Which of the following can easily see in the night?
(a) Owl   (b) Crow
(c) Parrot   (d) Sparrow

10. Which animal lives in place shown in the picture?

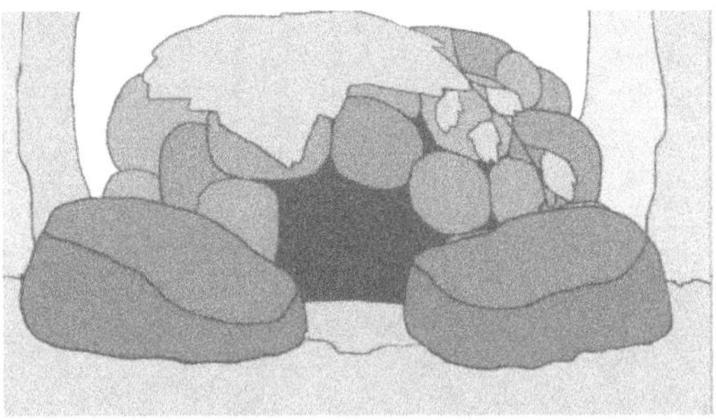

(a) Sheep   (b) Lion
(c) Giraffe   (d) Dog

11. Which of the following aquatic animals can live in water as well as on land?
(a) Fish   (b) Dolphin
(c) Turtles   (d) Whale

12. Which of the following pairs is not correctly matched?
(a) Domestic animal - Cow   (b) Wild animal - Elephant
(c) Water animal - Monkey   (d) Pet animal - Dog

13. Which of these animal lives in the Burrow?
(a) Sheep   (b) Tiger
(c) Spider   (d) Rabbit

14. Match the animals with their food.

Animals	Foods
A. Tiger	1. Sugarcane
B. Elephant	2. Grass
C. Rabbit	3. Flesh
D. Goat	4. Carrot

Codes

	A	B	C	D			A	B	C	D
(a)	1	2	3	4		(b)	4	3	2	1
(c)	3	1	4	2		(d)	2	1	4	3

15. Which of the following is kept in the cage shown below?

    (a) Fish   (b) Parrot   (c) Cat   (d) Dog

16. The penguin and polar bear live in ....

    (a) Desert   (b) Water   (c) Ice Region   (d) Mountains

17. Match the following animals with their sound.

Animals	Make Sound
A. Cat	1. Caw
B. Lion	2. Baa
C. Sheep	3. Meow
D. Crow	4. Roar

Codes

	A	B	C	D			A	B	C	D
(a)	3	4	2	1		(b)	4	2	1	3
(c)	2	3	4	1		(d)	1	2	3	4

18. Which animal spins a web for making its own house?

    (a) Sparrow   (b) Spider

    (c) Crab   (d) Owl

19. Which of the following is called the 'ship of the desert'?

    (a) Giraffe   (b) Crow

    (c) Camel   (d) Elephant

20. Leather is made from the skin of which of the following animals?

    (a) Camel   (b) Pigeon

    (c) Ant   (d) Fish

21. Which animal makes the sound Neigh-Neigh?
    (a) Donkey   (b) Horse
    (c) Tiger   (d) Cow

22. The Kitten is the baby of which of the following animals?
    (a) Cat   (b) Pig
    (c) Snake   (d) Cow

23. Which of the following sound is made by Donkey?
    (a) Bark   (b) Roar
    (c) Moo   (d) Bray

24. Select the option that correctly fill the blank.

    Wild Animal: Wolf : : Water Animal : ....
    (a) Octopus   (b) Wolf
    (c) Spider   (d) Pigeon

25. Match the following.

Animals	Used For
A. Hen	1. Milk
B. Buffalo	2. Carry heavy load
C. Donkey	3. Wool
D. Sheep	4. Eggs

Codes

	A	B	C	D			A	B	C	D
(a)	4	1	2	3		(b)	1	2	3	4
(c)	3	2	1	4		(d)	2	4	3	1

Chapter 13

Computers

1. The famous scientist Charles Babbage is also known as............ .
   (a) Father of Television
   (b) Father of Books
   (c) Father of Computer
   (d) Father of Internet

2. Which one of the following is an output device?
   (a) Mouse
   (b) Keyboard
   (c) Monitor
   (d) Scanner

3. What does 'P' stands for, in the terms of CPU?
   (a) Power
   (b) Position
   (c) Playback
   (d) Processing

4. The computer we use in our homes is also known as ....
   (a) Mini computer
   (b) Personal computer
   (c) Private computer
   (d) Business computer

5. Which of these is not a part of computer?

(a) 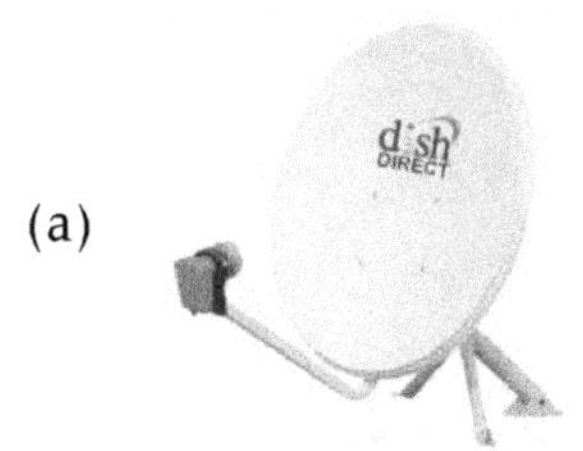

(b) 

(c) 

(d) 

6. By using which of the following will you give input to computer?
   (a) Keyboard
   (b) Printer
   (c) Monitor
   (d) Speaker

7. You can store your data in which of the following device?
   (a) Pen drive
   (b) Mouse
   (c) Monitor
   (d) Both (a) and (b)

8. In which of the following places computer is used?
   (a) Banks
   (b) Airport
   (c) Railway Station
   (d) All of these

9. Which one of the following is an audio device?
   (a) Monitor
   (b) Speakers
   (c) Mouse
   (d) CPU

10. Which of the following activity can we perform by using the given device?

    (a) Record video
    (b) Record voice
    (c) Listen to music
    (d) Play games

11. Which one of the following is associated with left click, right click and scrolling?
    (a) Mouse
    (b) Keyboard
    (c) Printer
    (d) Joystick

12. Which of the following activity you cannot do without Internet?
    (a) Listening music
    (b) Playing games
    (c) Searching on google
    (d) Painting

13. Which one of the following key is the biggest key in keyboard?
    (a) Caps lock key
    (b) Shift Key
    (c) Space key
    (d) Backspace key

14. Find the odd one out from the given options.
    (a) Google
    (b) Yahoo
    (c) Facebook
    (d) Recycle Bin

15. The part of computer shown in the image is used for which purpose?

(a) Listening to music   (b) Watching movies
(c) Storing data   (d) Typing

16. Which of the following activity can be done by using Internet?
(a) Bill Payment   (b) Watching online movies
(c) Video call   (d) All of these

17. Which one of the following is not a basic device of computer?
(a) Headphones   (b) Mouse
(c) Keyboard   (d) Monitor

18. Which one of the following cannot be done by computer?
(a) It can store data.   (b) It can take its own decision.
(c) It can be shut down.   (d) It can calculate faster

19. Where will you find the icons in the computer?
(a) On Keyboard   (b) On Printer
(c) On Screen   (d) On CPU

20. Which of the following computers can be carried from one place to another?
(a) Personal computer   (b) Laptop
(c) Super computer   (d) Sonic computer

21. What is the right way to close the computer?
(a) Close the switch   (b) Remove the wires
(c) By shutdown key   (d) By Restart Key

Chapter 14

Books and Authors

1. Which of the following book is written by J.K. Rowling?
   (a) The Jungle Book
   (b) Harry Potter
   (c) Anand Math
   (d) Broken Wings

2. The book, 'Playing it My Way' is written by........... .
   (a) Sachin Tendulkar
   (b) Sourav Ganguly
   (c) Virat Kohli
   (d) Rohit Sharma

3. The book 'Discovery of India' is written by........... .
   (a) Mahatma Gandhi
   (b) Sardar Patel
   (c) Jawaharlal Nehru
   (d) None of these

4. Which one of the following books is written by Narendra Modi?
   (a) Panchtantra
   (b) Kesari
   (c) Exam Warriors
   (d) Godan

5. Which of the following is the writer of the book 'The Jungle Book'?
   (a) Sarojini Naidu
   (b) J K Rowling
   (c) Rudyard Kipling
   (d) Kautilya

6. Which of the following books is written by Bankim Chandra Chatterjee?
   (a) Discovery of India
   (b) My Experiment with Truth
   (c) Anand Math
   (d) Panchtantra

7. The famous book "Two States" is written by
   (a) Kiran Bedi
   (b) Chetan Bhagat
   (c) Shashi Tharoor
   (d) Mahatma Gandhi

8. Which one of the following books is an autobiography of Mahatma Gandhi?
   (a) Discovery of India
   (b) Runs in Ruins
   (c) Bunch of Old Letters
   (d) My Experiment with Truth

9. Who had written the epic 'Ramayana'?
   (a) Rishi Valmiki
   (b) Ved Vyasa
   (c) Rishi Vashistha
   (d) Parashurama

10. Which one of the following books is written by our former President A P J Abdul Kalam?
    (a) The Broken Wings   (b) Wings of Water
    (c) Wings of Fire   (d) Conquest to Self

11. Which one of the following epics written by Ved Vyasa?
    (a) Mahabharata   (b) Ramayana
    (c) Vishnu Puran   (d) Godan

12. Who is the writer of the famous novel 'Hamlet'?
    (a) Christina Lamb   (b) Enid Blyton
    (c) William Shakespeare   (d) Chetan Bhagat

13. Which one of the famous book is written by the author Jonathan Swift?
    (a) Winnie The Pooh   (b) The Snow White
    (c) Cinderella   (d) Gulliver's Travels

14. Which one of the following is the writer of the book 'Panchtantra'?
    (a) Jawaharlal Nehru   (b) Sardar Patel
    (c) Chetan Bhagat   (d) Vishnu Sharma

15. The 'Ramcharitmanas' is written by
    (a) Surdas   (b) Tulsidas
    (c) Ramdas   (d) Ved Vyasa

16. The Book, 'Winnie-the-Pooh' was written by ....
    (a) Rudyard Kipling   (b) Roald Dahl
    (c) J K Rowling   (d) A A Milne

Chapter 15

Sports

1. What is the national game of our country?
   (a) Cricket   (b) Hockey   (c) Kabaddi   (d) Football

2. How many players can play a game of Chess at a single time?
   (a) 1   (b) 2   (c) 3   (d) 4

3. Which one of the following is not an indoor game?
   (a) Carrom   (b) Ludo   (c) Chess   (d) Cricket

4. The given image depicts which of the following sports?

   (a) Basketball   (b) Cricket
   (c) Football   (d) Volleyball

5. The equipments like- HELMET, BAT, GLOVES are used in which sports?
   (a) Basketball   (b) Cricket
   (c) Football   (d) Volleyball

6. Which of the following sport uses a net?
   (a) Lawn Tennis   (b) Volleyball
   (c) Badminton   (d) All of these

7. Which of the following sports is played without ball?
   (a) Badminton   (b) Basketball
   (c) Volleyball   (d) Hockey

8. Identify the sports personality shown in the picture

(a) Dhyan Chand   (b) Sardara Singh
(c) Baichung Bhutia   (d) Harbhajan Singh

9. Which one of the following sports is played by the help of air guns?
(a) Shooting   (b) Swimming
(c) Polo   (d) Hockey

10. The picture of the stick shown below belongs to which sports?

(a) Cricket   (b) Hockey
(c) Football   (d) Volleyball

11. How many stumps are used during a Cricket match?
(a) Four   (b) Five   (c) Six   (d) Three

12. The sportsperson shown in the image is related with which sports?

(a) Gymnastics   (b) Wrestling   (c) Boxing   (d) Football

13. Which of the following equipment is not required to play Volleyball?
  (a) Net (b) Court
  (c) Ball (d) Bat

14. The given court represent which of the following sports?

  (a) Hockey (b) Football
  (c) Badminton (d) Swimming

15. If "UMPIRE" is related to "CRICKET", then "REFEREE" is related to......... .
  (a) Chess (b) Football
  (c) Ludo (d) Hide and Seek

16. Identify the sport shown in the picture given below.

  (a) Gymnastics (b) Judo
  (c) Tennis (d) Basketball

17. How many kings are there in a game of chess?
  (a) 2 (b) 3 (c) 1 (d) 4

18. Which one of the following sportspersons is not related to Cricket?
  (a) Sachin Tendulkar (b) Virat Kohli
  (c) Abhinav Bindra (d) Rohit Sharma

19. Saina Nehwal is related to which sports?
  (a) Cricket (b) Hockey
  (c) Boxing (d) Badminton

20. Which of the following pairs is not correctly matched?
(a) Sunil Chhetri- Volleyball
(b) Mary Kom- Boxing
(c) Vishwanathan Anand- Chess
(d) Rahul Dravid- Cricket

21. Which of the following personalities is related to the sports 'Wrestling'?
(a) Sania Mirza
(b) Geeta Phogat
(c) Hima Das
(d) Saina Nehwal

22. .... is an Indian sprinter from the state of Assam. It is also known as "Dhing Express".
(a) Hima Das
(b) Babita Phogat
(c) PV Sindhu
(d) Babita Kumari

23. Identify the sportsperson shown in the image.

(a) MS Dhoni
(b) Yuvraj Singh
(c) Virat Kohli
(d) Rohit Sharma

Important Days and Dates

1. World Health Day is celebrated on which date?
(a) 14th February
(b) 7th April
(c) 1st January
(d) 31st December

2. Independence Day is celebrated in India on which date?
(a) 31st December
(b) 15th August
(c) 26th January
(d) 2nd October

3. Every year 26th January is celebrated as ....
(a) Republic Day
(b) Independence Day
(c) Gandhi Jayanti
(d) Christmas Day

4. Which Day is celebrated to give tribute to Father of the Nation?
(a) Children's Day
(b) Gandhi Jayanti
(c) Republic Day
(d) Independence Day

5. National Unity Day is celebrated on which date?
(a) 2nd October
(b) 31st October
(c) 1st January
(d) 31st December

6. On which of the following date, the Earth Day is celebrated ?
(a) 18th April
(b) 23rd April
(c) 31st April
(d) 22nd April

7. .... is celebrated on 5th June every year for the protection of the environment.
(a) World Heritage Day
(b) English Language Day
(c) World Environment Day
(d) World Science Day

8. 2nd October is celebrated as the .... all around the world.
(a) International Day of Non-Violence
(b) Father's Day
(c) Republic Day
(d) Independence Day

9. Every year 14th November is celebrated as.............. .
   (a) Teacher's Day   (b) Children's Day
   (c) Mother's Day   (d) Father's Day

10. 5th September is celebrated in India as ....
    (a) Doctors Day   (b) Air Force Day
    (c) Teachers Day   (d) Mothers Day

11. The Principal of school gives speech on the importance of water. The students make a posters on water usage to celebrate the ....
    (a)World Ozone Day   (b) World Earth Day
    (c) Independence Day   (d) World Water Day

12. Students along with teachers are planting trees in the school ground. According to you, which day are they celebrating?
    (a) World Environment Day   (b) English Language Day
    (c) World Science Day   (d) World Water Day

PRACTICE SET 01

1. If we fall ill, who gives us medicines, so that we can become healthy?
   (a) Doctor
   (b) Engineer
   (c) Policeman
   (d) Postman

2. Which one of the following planets is the biggest planet in our Solar System?
   (a) Mars
   (b) Saturn
   (c) Jupiter
   (d) Earth

3. The capital of Maharashtra is
   (a) Patna
   (b) Delhi
   (c) Kanpur
   (d) Mumbai

4. Which one of the following personalities has never been the Prime Minister of India?
   (a) A P J Abdul Kalam
   (b) Atal Bihari Vajpayee
   (c) Manmohan Singh
   (d) Jawaharlal Nehru

5. The tools shown in the image are used by which of the following?

   (a) Plumber
   (b) Mechanic
   (c) Doctor
   (d) Musician

6. The 'Guru Granth Sahib' is the holy book of which of the following religions?
   (a) Hindu
   (b) Sikhs
   (c) Muslims
   (d) Christians

7. In which of the following states, Pushkar Mela is held every year?
   (a) Haryana
   (b) Karnataka
   (c) Kerala
   (d) Rajasthan

8. Which one of the following instruments is associated with Goddess Saraswati?
(a) Guitar
(b) Violin
(c) Veena
(d) Tabla

9. 'The Palace of Wind' is located in which of the following states?
(a) Rajasthan
(b) Kerala
(c) Goa
(d) Tamil Nadu

10. Which one of the following organs is considerd as internal organ of our body?
(a) Tongue
(b) Nails
(c) Chest
(d) Liver

11. Which one of the following food items is made from milk?
(a) Fish
(b) Potato
(c) Curd
(d) Egg

12. Match the following.

List I (Food)		List II (Source)
A. Orange	1.	Hen
B. Sugar	2.	Cow
C. Milk	3.	Sugarcane
D. Eggs	4.	Plant

Codes

	A	B	C	D			A	B	C	D
(a)	1	3	2	4		(b)	4	3	2	1
(c)	2	3	4	1		(d)	1	2	3	4

13. The baby of which of the animal is known as Kid?
(a) Rabbit
(b) Horse
(c) Donkey
(d) Goat

14. Which of the following things are provided by plants?
(a) Cereals
(b) Coffee
(c) Vegetables
(d) All of these

15. Which of the following activities can we perform on our computer?
(a) Watching movies
(b) Painting
(c) Searching on Internet
(d) All of these

16. Which one of the following book is written by Bankim Chandra Chatterjee?
(a) Godan
(b) Anandmath
(c) Mahabharat
(d) Panchtantra

17. Gandhi Jayanti is celebrated every year on which of the following date?
  (a) 1st October   (b) 31st December
  (c) 2nd October   (d) 1st January

18. Which of the following sport uses a bigger ball than the others?
  (a) Cricket   (b) Golf   (c) Football   (d) Hockey

19. Identify the famous sportsperson shown in the picture.

  (a) Sania Mirza   (b) Saina Nehwal
  (c) Mary Kom   (d) Mithali Raj

20. Our planet Earth is also known as........ .
  (a) Red planet   (b) Pink planet   (c) Green planet   (d) Blue planet

21. Which one of the following is the newest Union Territory of India?
  (a) Ladakh   (b) Jammu and Kashmir
  (c) Puducherry   (d) Both (a) and (b)

22. The first woman President of our country is ....
  (a) Indira Gandhi   (b) Sarojini Naidu
  (c) Pratibha Patil   (d) Annie Besant

23. The given flag is associated with which of the following country?

  (a) Australia   (b) Brazil   (c) China   (d) New Zealand

24. Goddess Durga is worshipped in which festival?
   (a) Holi
   (b) Navaratri
   (c) Bihu
   (d) Ganesh Chaturthi

25. Which one of the following is the famous dance form of Kerala?
   (a) Kathakali
   (b) Mohiniattam
   (c) Garba
   (d) Both (a) and (b)

26. Which musical instrument is shown in the picture given below?

   (a) Veena
   (b) Sitar
   (c) Guitar
   (d) Piano

27. Which one of the following cities is known as 'Science City of India'?
   (a) Hyderabad
   (b) Chennai
   (c) Bengaluru
   (d) Shimla

28. Which organ pumps blood in our whole body?
   (a) Brain
   (b) Heart
   (c) Kidneys
   (d) Stomach

29. Which one of the following animals does NOT eat flesh?
   (a) Lion
   (b) Bear
   (c) Tiger
   (d) Cow

30. The cactus is a thorny plant which is found in ....
   (a) Hill areas
   (b) Desert areas
   (c) Water
   (d) Mud

31. Enter, Space and Caps Lock keys are found in which one of them?
   (a) Monitor
   (b) Mouse
   (c) Keyboard
   (d) CPU

32. Identify the personality shown in the picture is .... of India.

    (a) Prime Minister   (b) President
    (c) Chief Minister   (d) Vice-President

33. Which one of the following days is celebrated on 22nd April every year?
    (a) Water Day   (b) Earth Day
    (c) Independence Day   (d) Non-Violence Day

34. Which one of the following sports is associated with the personality Mary Kom?
    (a) Swimming   (b) Archery
    (c) Boxing   (d) Wrestling

35. We will not be able to listen anything, If we do not have ....
    (a) Eyes   (b) Ears
    (c) Nose   (d) Skin

PRACTICE SET  02

1. Which one of the following players is associated with Football?
   (a) Jasprit Bumrah   (b) Virat Kohli   (c) Dinesh Patel   (d) Sunil Chhetri

2. Identify the output device given below.

(a)    (b) 

(c)    (d) 

3. Find the odd one out from the given options.
   (a) Chess   (b) Billiards   (c) Volleyball   (d) Carrom

4. On which of the following dates Teacher's Day is celebrated every year?
   (a) 5th January   (b) 5th April   (c) 5th December   (d) 5th September

5. Identify the former Prime Minister of India shown in the image.

(a) Kiran Bedi   (b) Pratibha Patil   (c) Indira Gandhi   (d) Sarojini Naidu

6. Which of the following plants are used to make medicines?
   (a) Neem   (b) Tulsi
   (c) Mint   (d) All of these

7. Which of the following type of animals live in Jungle?
   (a) Pet animals   (b) Domestic animals
   (c) Water animals   (d) Wild animals

8. Pulses are a good source of ....
   (a) Carbohydrates   (b) Proteins
   (c) Fats   (d) Vitamins

9. Which one of the following organs is responsible for decision making, thinking and learning?
   (a) Heart   (b) Hairs
   (c) Stomach   (d) Brain

10. The tallest building 'Burj Khalifa' is located in which of the following countries?
    (a) United States of America   (b) United Kingdom
    (c) Russia   (d) United Arab Emirates

11. We can see a beautiful rainbow in the sky with the help of which organ?
    (a) Node   (b) Eyes
    (c) Ears   (d) Lips

12. In which of the following religions, people worship Lord Jesus?
    (a) Muslim   (b) Jainism
    (c) Christian   (d) Sikhs

13. Identify the country from the given flag.

(a) U S A   (b) Russia   (c) China   (d) Pakistan

14. Which dance form is shown in the picture given below?

    (a) Bhangra   (b) Bharatanatyam   (c) Kathakali   (d) Manipuri

15. Which one of the following states of India is located in the Eastern part of India?
    (a) Gujarat   (b) Tamil Nadu   (c) Uttar Pradesh   (d) West Bengal

16. Which one of the planets of the Solar System is made up of Gases?
    (a) Mercury   (b) Earth   (c) Venus   (d) Saturn

17. In which of the following places will you go to study and learn new things?
    (a) Restaurant   (b) School   (c) Park   (d) Market

18. Which of the following sports is being played by a ball and a racket?
    (a) Badminton   (b) Cricket   (c) Hockey   (d) Tennis

19. What does 'C' stands for in the full form of CPU?
    (a) Control   (b) Collect   (c) Central   (d) Common

20. Which of the following days is celebrated on 5th June every year for the protection of our surroundings?
    (a) World Heritage Day   (b) English Language Day
    (c) World Environment Day   (d) World Science Day

21. The book 'Exam Warrior' is written by which of the following personalities?
    (a) Jawaharlal Nehru   (b) Indira Gandhi   (c) A P J Abdul Kalam   (d) Narendra Modi

22. Which one of the following does not come under the category of a tree?
    (a) Rose   (b) Coconut   (c) Banyan   (d) Mango

23. Which of the following parts of plant provides support to upper parts of the plant?
    (a) Root   (b) Stem   (c) Leaves   (d) Flowers

24. Which of the following animals makes a sound 'Croak'?
    (a) Pig   (b) Cow   (c) Frog   (d) Dog

25. Which one of the following items can be eaten raw, without cooking?
    (a) Brinjal   (b) Potato   (c) Pumpkin   (d) Mango

26. Which one of the following is located in the upper part of the body?
    (a) Shoulder   (b) Foot   (c) Toe   (d) Knee

27. The city of Hyderabad is famous for which of the following monuments?
    (a) Qutub Minar   (b) Taj Mahal   (c) Sanchi Stupa   (d) Char Minar

28. Which one of the following is not the notes of sur in Hindustani music?
    (a) Sa   (b) Re   (c) Ga   (d) Ri

29. Which one of the following festivals is celebrated by our Muslim friends at the end of the fasting month of Ramadan?
    (a) Eid ul-Fitr   (b) Holi   (c) Onam   (d) Navaratri

30. The city 'Canberra' is the capital of which of the following country?
    (a) China   (b) Japan   (c) Brazil   (d) Australia

31. The famous leader Sarvepalli Radhakrishnan was the first .... of India.
    (a) Prime Minister   (b) Home Minister   (c) President   (d) Vice-President

32. Find the odd one out from the given options.
    (a) Bihar   (b) Patna   (c) Indore   (d) Lucknow

33. What is the position of the planet Earth from the Sun?
    (a) Second   (b) Fourth   (c) Sixth   (d) Third

34. Which one of the following makes wooden tables and chairs for our homes?
    (a) Mechanic   (b) Painter   (c) Carpenter   (d) Electrician

35. Identify the famous sportsperson shown in the picture.

    (a) Virat Kohli   (b) Hardik Pandya
    (c) Rohit Sharma   (d) Harbhajan Singh

Answers

Chapter 1   Our Surroundings

1. (c)	**2.** (d)	**3.** (c)	**4.** (c)	**5.** (b)	**6.** (a)	**7.** (b)	**8.** (b)	**9.** (b)	**10.** (a)
11. (d)	**12.** (d)	**13.** (c)	**14.** (a)	**15.** (d)	**16.** (a)	**17.** (d)	**18.** (d)	**19.** (c)	**20.** (b)
21. (d)	**22.** (c)	**23.** (a)							

Chapter 2   Solar System

1. (b)	**2.** (b)	**3.** (c)	**4.** (b)	**5.** (a)	**6.** (a)	**7.** (b)	**8.** (a)	**9.** (d)	**10.** (a)
11. (d)	**12.** (d)	**13.** (c)	**14.** (a)	**15.** (b)	**16.** (c)	**17.** (b)	**18.** (d)	**19.** (a)	**20.** (a)
21. (a)	**22.** (a)	**23.** (b)	**24.** (c)	**25.** (b)					

Chapter 3   My Country

1. (b)	**2.** (b)	**3.** (d)	**4.** (b)	**5.** (c)	**6.** (b)	**7.** (c)	**8.** (d)	**9.** (a)	**10.** (b)
11. (d)	**12.** (c)	**13.** (a)	**14.** (c)	**15.** (b)	**16.** (d)	**17.** (d)	**18.** (d)	**19.** (c)	**20.** (d)
21. (a)	**22.** (d)	**23.** (c)	**24.** (d)	**25.** (c)					

Chapter 4   Our President, PMs and CMs

1. (d)	**2.** (a)	**3.** (d)	**4.** (d)	**5.** (c)	**6.** (c)	**7.** (d)	**8.** (c)	**9.** (b)	**10.** (b)
11. (a)	**12.** (b)	**13.** (b)	**14.** (a)	**15.** (b)	**16.** (c)	**17.** (d)	**18.** (c)		

Chapter 5   Country; Capital and Flag

1. (c)	**2.** (b)	**3.** (d)	**4.** (a)	**5.** (b)	**6.** (b)	**7.** (c)	**8.** (b)	**9.** (a)	**10.** (b)
11. (a)	**12.** (a)	**13.** (c)	**14.** (c)	**15.** (a)	**16.** (c)	**17.** (c)	**18.** (c)	**19.** (d)	

Chapter 6   Fairs, Festivals and Religion

1. (a)	**2.** (d)	**3.** (b)	**4.** (d)	**5.** (d)	**6.** (a)	**7.** (c)	**8.** (d)	**9.** (b)	**10.** (c)
11. (b)	**12.** (b)	**13.** (c)	**14.** (d)	**15.** (b)	**16.** (c)	**17.** (b)	**18.** (b)	**19.** (a)	**20.** (b)
21. (a)	**22.** (c)	**23.** (d)	**24.** (c)	**25.** (b)	**26.** (b)	**27.** (c)	**28.** (c)		

Chapter 7   Music and Dance

1. (b)	**2.** (d)	**3.** (b)	**4.** (c)	**5.** (a)	**6.** (d)	**7.** (d)	**8.** (b)	**9.** (a)	**10.** (b)
11. (a)	**12.** (d)	**13.** (a)	**14.** (b)	**15.** (c)	**16.** (a)	**17.** (b)	**18.** (b)	**19.** (c)	**20.** (a)
21. (b)	**22.** (d)	**23.** (a)	**24.** (a)	**25.** (d)					

Chapter 8   Famous Places

1. (a)	2. (d)	3. (c)	4. (d)	5. (c)	6. (d)	7. (d)	8. (d)	9. (c)	10. (b)
11. (d)	12. (d)	13. (c)	14. (c)	15. (b)	16. (b)	17. (a)	18. (a)	19. (a)	20. (d)
21. (d)	22. (c)	23. (b)	24. (a)						

Chapter 9   Human Body

1. (a)	2. (b)	3. (a)	4. (d)	5. (a)	6. (c)	7. (d)	8. (a)	9. (d)	10. (d)
11. (b)	12. (d)	13. (b)	14. (c)	15. (d)	16. (d)	17. (c)	18. (d)	19. (d)	20. (a)
21. (d)	22. (d)	23. (a)	24. (c)						

Chapter 10   Food

1. (a)	2. (c)	3. (d)	4. (b)	5. (c)	6. (c)	7. (a)	8. (b)	9. (a)	10. (d)
11. (b)	12. (b)	13. (c)	14. (c)	15. (d)	16. (b)	17. (b)	18. (c)	19. (b)	20. (b)

Chapter 11   Plants

1. (a)	2. (c)	3. (d)	4. (c)	5. (b)	6. (a)	7. (c)	8. (d)	9. (d)	10. (b)
11. (b)	12. (b)	13. (b)	14. (b)	15. (d)	16. (b)	17. (b)	18. (d)	19. (b)	20. (c)
21. (b)	22. (a)	23. (c)	24. (a)	25. (d)	26. (d)	27. (d)			

Chapter 12   Animals

1. (b)	2. (d)	3. (c)	4. (b)	5. (a)	6. (b)	7. (c)	8. (d)	9. (a)	10. (b)
11. (c)	12. (c)	13. (d)	14. (c)	15. (b)	16. (c)	17. (a)	18. (b)	19. (c)	20. (a)
21. (b)	22. (a)	23. (d)	24. (a)	25. (a)					

Chapter 13   Computers

1. (c)	2. (c)	3. (d)	4. (b)	5. (a)	6. (a)	7. (a)	8. (d)	9. (b)	10. (a)
11. (a)	12. (c)	13. (c)	14. (c)	15. (c)	16. (d)	17. (a)	18. (b)	19. (c)	20. (b)
21. (c)									

Chapter 14   Books and Authors

1. (b)	2. (a)	3. (c)	4. (c)	5. (c)	6. (c)	7. (b)	8. (d)	9. (a)	10. (c)
11. (a)	12. (c)	13. (d)	14. (d)	15. (b)	16. (d)				

Chapter 15   Sports

1. (b)	**2.** (b)	**3.** (d)	**4.** (a)	**5.** (b)	**6.** (d)	**7.** (a)	**8.** (b)	**9.** (a)	**10.** (b)
11. (c)	**12.** (c)	**13.** (d)	**14.** (c)	**15.** (b)	**16.** (a)	**17.** (a)	**18.** (c)	**19.** (d)	**20.** (a)
21. (b)	**22.** (a)	**23.** (b)							

Chapter 16   Important Days and Dates

1. (b)	**2.** (b)	**3.** (a)	**4.** (b)	**5.** (b)	**6.** (d)	**7.** (c)	**8.** (a)	**9.** (b)	**10.** (c)
11. (d)	**12.** (a)								

Practice Set 1

1. (a)	**2.** (c)	**3.** (d)	**4.** (a)	**5.** (b)	**6.** (b)	**7.** (d)	**8.** (c)	**9.** (a)	**10.** (d)
11. (c)	**12.** (b)	**13.** (d)	**14.** (d)	**15.** (d)	**16.** (b)	**17.** (c)	**18.** (c)	**19.** (b)	**20.** (d)
21. (d)	**22.** (c)	**23.** (a)	**24.** (b)	**25.** (d)	**26.** (c)	**27.** (c)	**28.** (b)	**29.** (d)	**30.** (b)
31. (c)	**32.** (b)	**33.** (b)	**34.** (c)	**35.** (b)					

Practice Set 2

1. (d)	**2.** (c)	**3.** (c)	**4.** (d)	**5.** (c)	**6.** (d)	**7.** (d)	**8.** (b)	**9.** (d)	**10.** (d)
11. (b)	**12.** (c)	**13.** (c)	**14.** (c)	**15.** (d)	**16.** (d)	**17.** (b)	**18.** (d)	**19.** (c)	**20.** (c)
21. (d)	**22.** (a)	**23.** (b)	**24.** (c)	**25.** (d)	**26.** (a)	**27.** (d)	**28.** (d)	**29.** (a)	**30.** (d)
31. (d)	**32.** (a)	**33.** (d)	**34.** (c)	**35.** (c)					